Poetic Justice

Poetic Justice

Written by Fraser Sampson

Illustrated by Desmond Harry Keys

Wise Owl Books

Wise Owl Books
An imprint of HLT Publications
200 Greyhound Road, London W14 9RY

First published 1990 © The HLT Group Ltd

ISBN 1 85353 903 6

British Library Cataloguing-in-Publication.

A CIP Catalogue record for this book is available from the British Library.

Printed and bound in Great Britain.

Contents

A Dash of Rum

When making a trawl
For the Court's Christmas Ball
The Usher was seeking donations.
He'd all types of fare
And gifts everywhere
From chocolates to tree decorations.
Then the Clerk said, "I think
I'll contribute some drink,
As it's this time of year I'd be glad to.
Do you think we could run
To a litre of rum?"
Said the Usher, "I'd crawl if I had to!"

Capital Punishment

Mr Sydney Silverman
In 1964
Introduced a famous Bill
That soon became the law.

Hanging was abolished
As an option for the Court
When sentencing for murder
And offences of that sort.

Hoorah for British Justice!
Exemplar of the time
Civilized and sanitized
Enlightened and benign.

But penal progress hasn't gone
As Silverman proposed
The drop's alive
And kicking
With the sentence self-imposed.

That barbarous chastisement
Relinquished by the state
Transformed from final sanction
Into ultimate escape.

A suffocating system
Stifles Britain's misspent youth
Where sheets and shirts and shoestrings
Now supplant the hangman's noose.

The General Eyre

When came the dreaded General Eyre
With courts of Nisi Prius
The Cornish Chiefs cried 'Don't despair
These things are sent to try us!'

The General Eyre - an explanatory note

Under the Statute of Westminster was enacted the first general provision for common law actions on issues of fact to be tried on circuit. The Statute required the Sheriff to summon jurors to Westminster to hear cases set down for trial 'unless before' (or *nisi prius*) the circuit judges on assize had visited the defendant's county.

Of these *nisi prius* courts, one very important commission of itinerant justices was the 'General Eyre' who would visit counties every five or seven years and hold a protracted inquisition into every aspect of their affairs. The General Eyre was, not unnaturally perhaps, very unpopular and in 1233 the men of Cornwall are reputed to have fled to the woods rather than face these powerful royal justices …

Diplomatic Immunity

Breaking the law with impunity
Political games can be cruel
Diplomatic immunity
Britannia waives the rules.

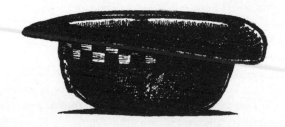

Grave Misgivings

Whilst walking through a graveyard
I one day chanced upon
A tiny granite gravestone
With these few words thereon:

"A lawyer and an honest man
Lieth in this tomb"
Two men in one small grave, I thought,
I can't see how there's room.

Judicial Jokes

Two famous Law Lords from our highest courts
Were perusing a page of the Times Law Reports
The judgements, they felt, were too dull and too terse
The grammar was bad and the syntax was worse.

Said one, "What became of those judicial jokes
Which so entertained all we judicial folks?"
Said the other, "They've left us forever I feel
Though some say they sit in the Court of Appeal!"

All 'E Rote!

The learned reporter, notebook in hand
Rushed out of the Chancery Courts
But a student of law was lying in wait
To ambush the fresh law reports.

"Anything int'resting happen today?"
Beseeched the importunate voice
"You'd never believe it" the barrister gasped
"So much one was spoiled for choice!"

"Treason, corruption and murder most foul
Were committed right here in this Court
And that's not the best",
Cried the student: "You jest"
"Well you started it," came the retort.

Confinement

Mary had a baby
She called him Sonny Jim
Mary went to Woolworths
And stole some clothes for him
Mary was imprisoned
For her petty little crime
Now mother and her baby boy
Are both doing time.

Smear Campaign

Saturation policing
Is like hard toilet paper, I've found
It doesn't wipe out the problem
But merely spreads it around.

Kleptomania

The Kleptomaniac's yen
Is to pinch things now and again
Not now and again
"Now and again"
But now,
And again
And again.

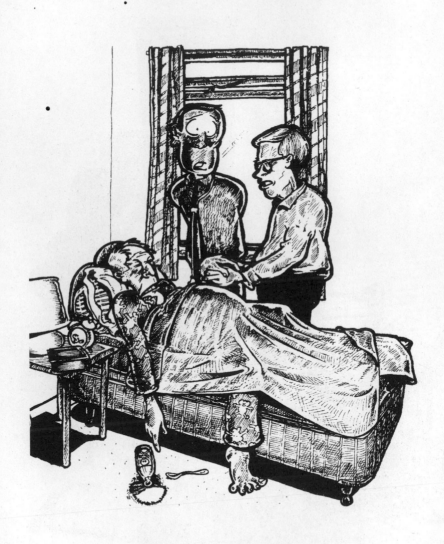

Malice Aforethought

The deceased, a doctor narrated
Was killed by some medicine he'd tasted
The Coroner conceded
An inquest was needed
As death had been pre-medicated.

Great Expectations

"I've just had my annual appraisal you know"
The gullible constable chirped.
"Promotion is only a matter of time
And my route to the top is a cert.
I read the Chief's comment, he wrote it himself
The inference couldn't be stronger
He says with my record I shouldn't expect
To stay a P.C. for much longer."

Where's the Sod in Justice?

A desolate Defendant
Found guilty as indicted
Believed the jury's verdict
Had left fair play unrequited

"There *is* no soddin' justice"
Wailed the prisoner poignantly
"Oh yes, young man, there is"
Replied the Judge, "and I am he!"

Alibi

An Alibi's a term of art
That's easy to define
It simply means that you were in
Two places at one time.

The Modern Day Chief Constable

I am the very model of a modern day Chief Constable
Concerned with the community for whom I am responsible
I hold an LLB and I've a first in criminology
I'm well-versed in man-management, religion and psychology
I am the very picture of Constabulary propriety
A paragon of virtue and a pillar of society
My lifestyle's ozone friendly and my diet vegetarian
My character unsullied and my views humanitarian
I advocate sobriety and promulgate morality
And make a great display of my political neutrality
In conference I'm competent, on TV I'm commendable
In times of national crisis I am solid and dependable
My only club is ACPO which helps keep Chiefs eudemonical
A little cabalistic yes, but never quite Masonical
But backing from the Home Department's what a poor Dep wants most of all
For otherwise he'll *never* be a modern day Chief Constable.

Judge in Chambers

(a tribute to Unelott J.)

Awake from blissful slumber deep
That only babes and judges sleep
His Lordship took a cautious peep
From underneath the covers

And entertaining happy thoughts
Of battles won, and lost, and fought
In endless days in countless courts
He rose to face another

But though he longed to join the fray
Of yet another judgement day
His bold but brittle back gave way
To years of courtroom strain

He pushed and pulled, and cussed and cursed
Which seemed to help a bit at first
But only made the problem worse
His efforts were in vain

He gave his wife a loving nudge
"My dear I simply cannot budge"
Bemoaned the rigid red-robed judge
Lain crumpled on the bed

Believing he'd alluded to
A case, as he was wont to do
His wife smiled, "Yes dear, good for you,
You stand your ground," she said

"I'm often badgered by defence
For some perceived intransigence
But right now in the literal sense
I *cannot* move," he sighed

At length the local doctor called
Subpoenaed to the judge's Hall
But he could do no good at all,
A long rest was prescribed

"The remedy this doctor seeks",
Opined the judge from 'neath the sheets
"Would keep me out of court for weeks
It's just a tricky back"

"If I'm to be confined to bed"
He plonked his wig down on his head
"I'll try the buggers here instead
And over-rule the quack!"

And so began the bedside trials
Of litigants who trekked for miles
Procured by those judicial wiles
That made our judges famous

And counsel brought their every case
To that great judge's sleeping place
From error on the record's face
To probate and mandamus

And breaking novel judging ground
Resplendent in red dressing gown
Upon a quilted eiderdown
His Lordship's court commenced

His learned clerk knelt at his feet
Solicitors grabbed the comfy seats
The shorthand writer sat en suite
And justice was dispensed

So, interrupted once or twice
By cups of tea and sound advice
Provided by his Lady wife
The brave man changed the rules

And there in front of court and co
His Lordship did his best to show
That Justice never sleeps, although
She's sometimes prone to snooze

But as the day drew to a close
The wise old judge began to doze
In judging that's the way it goes
And great men too get tired

His lady wife pulled down the blinds
And asked, "Would those assembled mind
Adjourning as I think you'll find
This court has now retired"

So counsel and the learned team
Had left the judge alone to dream
Of future court (or bed) room scenes
And new forensic dramas

The multitude then slipped away
Though none would quite forget the day
The High Court sat, or rather lay
Bedecked in silk pyjamas.

Mens Sana

Forlorn in the Dock of the local Crown Court
Stood a joiner's apprentice from Leeds
Whose counsel advised him
His one final hope
Was to show he was unfit to plead

A jury was sworn to determine the facts
Surrounding the lad's state of mind
Once counsel had shown his
Shortcomings to be
Merely those of a cerebral kind

Experts attested again and again
Condemning the hapless apprentice
Till all men of reason would
Have to agree
The poor boy was *non compos mentis*

But 'all men of reason' discounted the judge
A sceptical, cynical type
Who marked his dissention with
Fine terms of art
Such as 'piffle'! and 'twaddle'! and 'tripe'!

When counsel concluded his final address
The judge faced the jury and scowled
"From what I can see the
Poor man in the dock
Is as sane as I am," he growled.

Counsel rose slowly and feigned a low bow
As he said, in satirical tone
"I'm obliged to your honour for
Making that point
But I should win this case on my own."

Astronomical Vision

"Was it dark on that night?"
Defence counsel probed
"Yes, very," the Officer sighed.
"Just how far could you see?"
Counsel asked pointedly
"I could see the moon," he replied.

Going Begging

Getting bail from His Honour Judge Clegg
Was like kicking ass with one leg
Some, it was thought
Brought their dogs into court
As the best way to teach them to beg.

Percy's Peroration

- a cautionary tale -

Percy Shorley Boreham-Wood
Barrister-at-law
Began his peroration
Lasting several days or more

As Percy plodded onward
In soporific tone
The court became anaesthetized
By his incessant drone

The jury started drooping
The clerk began to doze
But Percy persevered with
His interminable prose

At length poor Percy noticed
A juror counting sheep
"I must protest your Honour"
Percy pointed, "He's asleep!"

The judge, who'd been presiding
In the higher courts of Nod
Was woken when a witness
Gave his arm a gentle prod

"Mr Boreham-Wood," he scowled
And shook his learned head
"You made the fellow dormant,
You wake him up," he said

"And may I beg of counsel
If there *is* to be an end
We get there in my lifetime
Or he'll have to start again."

"May I remind your honour"
Piped Percy purple-faced
"Counsel must have latitude
To fight his client's case!"

"And I would caution counsel"
His Honour wryly said
"That latitude's no problem
It's the longitude we dread!"

The Speed Trap

In a certain anonymous Magistrates' Court
A motorway constable stood
Giving his spiel
With a passionate zeal
As only a traffic man would.

Defence counsel wearily rose to his feet
And gave the old copper a leer
"How fast did you say
My client went on that day?"
He asked with a well-practised sneer.

"Around about eighty," came the reply
Prompting Counsel's incredulous shout
"Oh you've some special power
To compute miles per hour
As you've told us your speedo was out?"

"After twenty years service," he said with conviction
"My guess is as good as a reading
I've weighed, checked and towed
Every make on the road
And in my view that car was speeding."

"Right," Counsel said and flung his gold pen
Past their worships whose anger was showing
"It's only a small point
But you saw that ball point
Pray tell us, how fast was it going?"

The officer shrugged as he turned to the bench
Whose expressions became even darker
"I wouldn't profess
To hazard a guess
But then I've not driven a Parker!"

Blind Justice

The robber stood in the lonely dock
Wishing he had asked
What denier
Those stockings were
Before he'd used the mask.

Intoximeter

I got myself breathalysed four weeks ago
The policeman said, "Here's a new game,
It's a bag that turns pink
When you've had too much drink"
I said, "I've one at home just the same."

Tempus Fugit

My doctor gave me six months to live
My solicitor said, "No big deal
You can hold back the grief
I've sent counsel the brief
And he thinks that we've grounds for appeal."

The Crooked Man

There was a crooked man
Who walked a crooked mile
And found a crooked sixpence
Against a crooked stile
And for a crooked moment
His crooked world looked sunny
Till the crooked King decided
That the crooked can't have money.
He got a crooked policeman
To take the crooked man
To the crooked royal courtroom
That his crooked judges ran
There the crooked policeman
Gave a crooked tale
And so the crooked judges sent
The crooked man to jail.
"Just my crooked luck," he said
"To come a crooked cropper
And find a crooked sixpence
A Sovereign and a copper!"

Robbery Made Simple

Simple Simon met a pieman
Going to the fair.
Said Simple Simon to the pieman
"Let me taste your ware"
The threatened pieman feared that Simon
Would then and there use force
So, theft complete, young Simon's feat
Was robbery of course.

Right of Audience

To talk to our fabled Chief Constable
Is akin to Parole Board repentance
You swear there and then
Not to do it again
And you don't get to finish your sentence!

Little Jack Horner

Little Jack Horner
Sat in a corner
Eating a Christmas pie
He put in his thumb
Found a snail and yelled, "Mum
Does *Donoghue* v *Stevenson* apply?"

On the Cards

The Queen of Hearts she made some tarts
All on a summer's day
The Knave of Hearts he stole the tarts
And took them clean away.

The King of Hearts called for the tarts
And sent the Knave for trial
But yes, you guessed, the C.P.S.
Had lost another file …

Obscene but not Heard

A young heavy breather called Ferris
Phoned an elderly lawyer named Nerys
And though she mis-heard
A few vital words
She construed them *ejusdem generis*.

'Nemo me Impune Lacessit'
(Touch me not with impunity)

- For Chris C.

A civil rights lawyer from Troon
Took a colleague back to his room
They argued all night
Over who had the right
To do what, and with what, and to whom.

Reflective Practice

I broke an old mirror a fortnight ago
That's seven years' bad luck for sure
My brief said that's fine
With a record like mine
I'll probably get off with four!

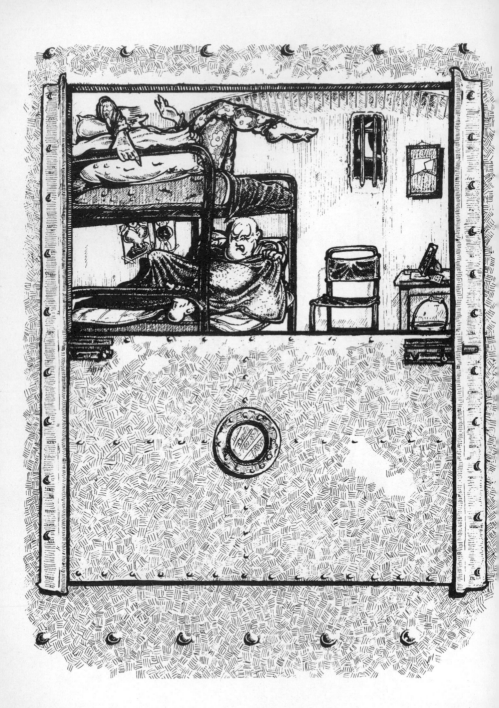

Cell Mates

'Neath Glasgow's infamous prison
Poor Wullie considered his fate
Two years in this grime
Seemed an awfy lang time
As the officer dead-locked the gate
He sat on his bunk and woefully sighed
"I've got to get oot o' Bar L
Still, my lawyer's appealing"
Then a voice near the ceiling
Said, "I know some cuties mysel'."

Bottom of the Class

The principal's message was clear
No charades in the classroom this year
Since two daring students
Of our jurisprudence
Gave a graphic display of *mens rea*.

Delusions of Grandeur

"Delusions of grandeur M'Lord," said the brief
"Are what brought this poor lady to court
Compelled to 'borrow' a bit here and there,
She'd extravagant needs to support."

"Quite so" said the judge peering down at the dock
As he gave an inscrutable smile
"Well then my dear
You'll go down for a year
Then you'll really be living in Styal."

Vehicular Vernacular

The bench asked the driver some questions
When the policeman had given his bit
On the terrible state of the vehicle
And the things that he'd found wrong with it
"Is your handbrake able to hold your car still?"
Asked the Chairman and then he looked up …
"… On the level?" he said
And the driver went red
"Yeah honest Guvnor, straight up!"

Law Inaction

Reeking Rotting Risley Remand
What dilatory code could inflict it?
If the law is an ass
Then from what I can see
It's about time somebody kicked it.

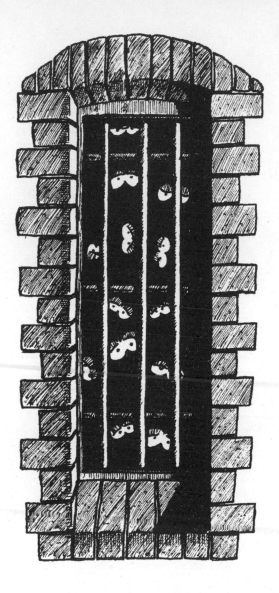

Byre Beware!

It was Christmas Eve in the farmyard
And the farmer was out in the shed
Trying to get milk from his old dairy cow
Before retiring to bed

But Daisy was just not in the moo-d
For twelve months now she had stuck it
The farmer was starting to get on her teats
So she deftly hoofed over his bucket

The farmer tried again and again
But was getting nowhere at all
So he finally tied poor Daisy's hind legs
To either side of her stall

"Come now old girl," said the farmer
As he re-positioned his pail
But just as he took hold of Daisy again
She upset the lot with her tail

The old man tied the tail to a rope
Which he flung up over a rafter
And hoisted the awkward appendage aloft
To get to the milk he was after

There the faithful old Friesian had stood
Her recalcitrant legs spread akimbo
With her four hooves firmly strapped to the floor
And her swishing tail strung up in limbo

At this point the drunken old herdsman
After guzzling beer through the day
Staggered around to the back of the barn
And gave his crops a quick spray

But as he came back to the cowshed
Clumsily buttoning his fly
He saw that the noise had attracted
A policeman who'd been cycling by

Well picture if you're able the scene
That greeted the good village copper
The drunken farmer closing his zip
Behind Daisy trussed up good and proper

The point that belies this quaint country scene
Though completely lost on the officer:
Thank goodness in English Criminal Law
The *res do NOT ipsa loquitur*.

Trivial Pursuit

In the People's Republic of Barnsley
The Magistrates' Court was in session
Their Worships were hearing
The latest lament
That their people had suffered repression

The Brief felt his client should not have been charged
With this 'paltry and venial' crime
(It seems he'd run over
A constable's cap
With a constable in at the time)

"Sergeant you're wasting the time of this court"
Said the lawyer concluding his case
"And next time your men
Step out in the road
They should first find a safe crossing place

"The law's not concerned with such trifles as these
If it were then we'd soon be bogged down
With all our policemen sitting in court
Instead of protecting our town

"Did you not think: *De minimis non curat lex*
Before hauling him off to the cells?"
The sergeant sardonically smiled at the Bench
"Oh yes Sir, we talked of nowt else."

Legal Aid

An articled clerk from Belgrade
Had misunderstood Legal Aid
Her law books she selled off
And sent to Bob Geldof
The pitiful sum she had made.

Strange Ways

Strangeways Oh Strangeways
What an apposite name,
All creature comforts complete.
You get warmed and fed
And a place for your head
And a good roof under your feet.

His Word is Your Bond

"The most basic of all a prisoner's rights"
Counsel lectured the Superintendent
"Is the one granting access to legal advice
The one you denied the defendant
And the reasons on which you based your decision
Don't meet the requirements of PACE
You seem to believe that your word would suffice
When clearly that isn't the case

"Did you think you could stand on your own *ipse dixit?*"
He laid on the melodramatics
Said the Super, "That date I'd enough on my plate
Without trying to do acrobatics."

59

In Two Minds

The charge was 'maliciously wounding'
The defendant a drunkard called Dew
The case had been brought
To the Magistrates' Court
Full committal, not section 6(2)

The P.C. had given his story
From notes that he'd made at the time
But the Beak seemed to think
That a surfeit of drink
Had been partly to blame for the crime

The Learned Stipe interrupted
Confusing the nervous young cop
"Had Dew had much to drink?"
The lad stopped to think
"No Your Worship, I'd not touched a drop!"

Dew's solicitor jumped to his feet,
The laughter had caused him concern
Such men as he
Saw no profit in glee
And he asked that the court should adjourn

Having failed, the lawyer then struggled to cite
A reason to end the committal
"Sir you will find
A disease of the mind
Must result in my client's acquittal

His personality's split into two
And alcohol's caused the divide
From a medical view
He's not one man but two
One Jekyll, the other one Hyde."

"Well I never," mused the wily old Beak
"That could cause me some problems with bail
So I shall decree
Doctor Jekyll goes free
But Hyde will, of course, go to jail."

(J.S.)

Much Ado About Nothing?

In London's fair city
Where girls are so pretty
As indeed are some of the men
A little old dear
Had a ticket to see a
Play in the famous West End

When the show was complete
She'd gone out in the street
To see who came through the stage door
But what a surprise
Entertained her old eyes
A performance she'd not bargained for!

A forward old chap
In a cloth cap and mac
Gave a brief but revealing display
In a public parade of
What he was made of
Bowed, and then scurried away

Well, shocked but unharmed
She had raised the alarm
And a constable entered stage right
With a note-book and pen
He asked what where and when
Was the cause of the old lady's fright

The man who'd attacked her
She said, was an actor
A truly *dramatis persona*
She told of the sight,
Of his build and his height
And the various things he had shown her

"The man that you saw,
Have you seen him before?"
Said the constable, making a start
She replied, "I should say
He appeared in that play
But he only had a small part."

(exeunt)

Corpus Delicti

In an overworked inner city Crown Court
The overdue case came to trial
But overweight counsel who led for the Crown
Had overlooked most of the file

The trial limped along in a tedious farce
And the judge had become quite distraught
Crown Counsel had clearly not covered the case
As competent Crown Counsel ought

"What harm did you say befell the complainant?"
Asked the judge as she thought of retiring
"I think that she'd fractured her acetubulum"
Stalled corpulent counsel perspiring

The judge sighed, "Would you enlighten the jury
By explaining that medical phrase?"
Bewigged and bewildered the bloated brief blushed
Beneath the disparaging gaze

"I'm afraid my anatomy's not all that good"
He blurted out the confession
Said the judge, "That I fear is patently clear
But would you explain the expression!"

The Cab Rank Rule

The Cab Rank Rule
Is designed to fool
Opponents of the English Bar

Of all Bar pranks
Then the Cab Rule Ranks
As probably the most bizarre

Next come, next served's
The cabbies' watchword
And one the Bar profess to share

But Rank Rules Cabs
Which are up for grabs
Provided you can find the fare

I've tried to view
This Rank Cab Rule
The way that we're supposed to do

But I place no faith
In a system based
On the ethics of a taxi queue.

Mirror, Mirror

Mirror, mirror on the wall
Who's the fairest of them all?

"British Justice I'd have thought"

Oh mirror, when last were you in court!

Justice is Good for You

In all our great British criminal courts
Ev'ryone's given a space
The seating you'll find
Is clearly designed
To ensure that we all know our place

Solicitors witnesses counsel and clerks
Each have their own little stall
Jurors, stenographers
Judges' biographers
Uncle Tom Cobley 'n' all

But most important of all is the Dock
Where defendants of all classes go
Till either side's won
And justice is done
And, moreover, is seen to be so

But not if you're corporate men of stout wealth,
Not for them such demeaning restraint
To some plutocrats
It's Pure Genius perhaps
But justice it certainly ain't.

Justice

Justice is fairness
Rectitude right
Justice is innocence, moral requite

Justice is equity
Honesty too
Justice is doing as gods bid us do

Justice is recompense
Making amends
Justice is getting your own back again

Justice is reasonable
Justice is true
Justice is getting what's coming to you

Justice is brutal
Justice is kind
Justice is decent, impartial and blind

Justice is equal
An eye for an eye
Justice is reason to wound, kill and die

Justice is wild and
Justice is rough
Justice is merciful, justice is tough

Justice is fickle
Poetic and plain
Justice is measured, it's weighed and it's strained

Justice is judgment
Divine retribution
Justice is destined, the final solution

Justice is nebulous
Vague and unseen
Justice is imminent, justice has been

Justice is personal
Private, subjective
Justice is relative, viewed in perspective

Justice is doubtful
Just what is just?
Justice is doing what laws say we must

Justice demands
It condemns and accuses
Justice legitimates, justice excuses

Justice prevails
It endures and it lives
Just what is justice? Justice just is!